VASCO DA GAMA

The Sea Route to India

Written by Thomas Melchers
In collaboration with Ludivine Péchoux
Translated by Rebecca Neal

History **50MINUTES**.com

VASCO DA GAMA — 1

Key information

Introduction

BIOGRAPHY — 3

In service of the Portuguese Crown

En route to Asia

The last expedition

POLITICAL, SOCIAL AND ECONOMIC CONTEXT — 7

Europe's conquest of the world

Portuguese sea expeditions

In search of India

THE EXPEDITIONS — 11

The first voyage (1497-1499)

The second voyage (1502-1503)

The last voyage (1524)

IMPACT — 20

A new organisation of trade

New power relationships in the Mediterranean

The Christianisation of India

A new knowledge of the world

SUMMARY — 23

FIND OUT MORE — 27

VASCO DA GAMA

KEY INFORMATION

- **Born:** 1460 or 1469 in Sines, Portugal.
- **Died:** 1524 in Cochin, India.
- **Aim of the expedition:** to discover a maritime route to India and find spices.
- **Regions of the world explored:**
    - First voyage (1497-1499): South Africa, Mozambique, Kenya, Somalia and India.
    - Second voyage (1502-1503): Mozambique, Kenya and India.
    - Third voyage (1524): India.
- **Main achievement:** the establishment of a direct maritime route from Europe to India and Asia by sailing around Africa.

INTRODUCTION

Along with Christopher Columbus (Genoese navigator, 1451-1506) and Ferdinand Magellan (Portuguese navigator, 1480-1521), Vasco da Gama is one of the most famous European explorers of his time. This Portuguese navigator was born in the 1460s and was the first person to open up a direct maritime route connecting Europe and Asia. After sailing around Africa, he reached the Western coast of India in the late 15th century, which had major consequences for the spice trade. Indeed, until the Fall of Constantinople in 1453, exotic goods, such as silk and some food products, had been transported to Europe by the Italian maritime republics which traded with Arab merchants. However, the growth of the Ottoman Empire and the rise in taxes on exchanges gradually jeopardised this trade, which drove the European nations to obtain spice supplies directly from their source.

This was the context in which Vasco da Gama embarked on his three maritime voyages to Asia and India. He had a diverse range of motivations, including in particular exploration, the defence of Portuguese interests and the administration of Portuguese India. Although he faced some obstacles on the way, he managed to lay the foundations of the Portuguese Empire by establishing several trading posts.

BIOGRAPHY

Portrait of Vasco da Gama by Antoine Maurin, c. 1835.

IN SERVICE OF THE PORTUGUESE CROWN

Vasco da Gama was born in either 1460 or 1469 in the small coastal village of Sines, south-west Portugal. His parents, Estêvão da Gama and Isabel Sodré, came from families of the lower Portuguese nobility and had three sons and a daughter.

When it was time to begin his studies, da Gama left his hometown for Évora in the south of Portugal. As a young man, he served the interests of the Portuguese Crown and took part in a series of conflicts in North Africa. In 1492, he led a small naval expedition, and five years later he was chosen to establish the first trade route to the Indies. It is difficult to determine precisely why he was chosen for this position, as only a small amount of information about his youth has survived.

EN ROUTE TO ASIA

In 1497, da Gama left Lisbon to establish a route to the Indies. It would take him 11 months to sail around Africa and arrive, in May 1498, at the south of the Indian peninsula. In Calicut, he met the Zamorin (local Hindu ruler and the man in charge of the spice trade), with whom he had a somewhat antagonistic relationship. In spite of these tensions, da Gama was able to load a large quantity of spices and precious stones into the holds of his ships, and returned to Lisbon in 1499, thus becoming the first navigator to travel between Europe and the Indian subcontinent by sea. As a result of this success, da Gama was awarded the title Admiral of the Seas of Arabia, Persia, India and all the Orient.

Vasco da Gama before the Zamorin of Calicut, painting by
Veloso Salgado, 1898.

In 1502, the king of Portugal, Manuel I (1469-1521), entrusted
da Gama with a new mission: to remove the competition
represented by Muslim merchants, to make the Zamorin of
Calicut yield to the Portuguese, and to form alliances with
rival cities. The explorer was therefore essentially setting
out on a conquest. To achieve this, da Gama had no qualms
about using force, which would damage his career and repu-
tation. He fell into disgrace and retired with his family to the
northern part of Portugal's Alentejo region.

THE LAST EXPEDITION

Da Gama did not lead another expedition to India until 1524. Having been restored to favour with the King of Portugal, he was appointed as the Portuguese Viceroy of India, where he was tasked with restoring the interests of the Crown, eradicating corruption and protecting the trading posts there. However, he died three months later, while the reforms in Portuguese India were underway, in this way preventing his enemies from stirring up any reversal of the situation.

Shortly after his death, he became a key historical figure in Portugal, thanks in particular to the many authors who praised his exploits, such as the poet Luís de Camões (1525-1580).

POLITICAL, SOCIAL AND ECONOMIC CONTEXT

EUROPE'S CONQUEST OF THE WORLD

The second half of the 15th century was a period of considerable change in Europe. Geopolitical changes and economic needs led several European countries to take to the Atlantic in search of new maritime routes and the abundant wealth of other nations. However, the element which triggered this European expansion was the Fall of Constantinople in 1453. In that year, Mehmed the Conqueror (Ottoman sultan, 1432-1481) conquered Constantinople and in this way precipitated the fall of the Byzantine Empire, a descendent of the Western Roman Empire. Although the consequences of the fall of the city could not be seen directly in the rest of Europe, that did not make them any less significant. Exotic goods (silk, dyes, spices, etc.) coming from the Indian Ocean were exported by Arab merchants in the ports of the Eastern Mediterranean and in Italian trading posts. However, the growth of the Ottoman Empire resulted in a constant increase in taxes on these products, leading some European countries to embark on expeditions in order to bypass the Arab intermediaries.

SPICES

One of the main motivations behind the Portuguese expeditions was the acquisition of spices. Although they had been known since Antiquity, cinnamon, ginger, nutmeg, cardamom, cloves and black pepper were considered to be luxury products at this time. Spices, which were used to mask the taste of poorly preserved meat and to produce medical remedies, were of an inestimable value for the countries that traded them.

However, spices were not the main reason for Portugal's maritime explorations. Like most European countries in the 15th century, Portugal was suffering from a shortage of precious metals. Silver from mines in Central Europe and gold from Guinea were no longer enough to satisfy needs linked to the demographic boom, commercial exchanges or growing military requirements. Consequently, Portugal needed to find a new source of precious metals and therefore embarked on the conquest of the Guinean coasts in order to supply itself with gold directly.

PORTUGUESE SEA EXPEDITIONS

One of the main reasons why Portugal was quick to embark on maritime exploration, in this way ushering in the era of great discoveries, was its geographical location. Being situated next to the Atlantic Ocean allowed sailors to gain substantial navigation experience. At the time, the Europeans were afraid of venturing out into the seas. In spite of the fears and other superstitions surrounding maritime expeditions, Portuguese sailors took to the sea in order to expand the borders of the known world.

From 1420 onwards, the second son of King John I (1357-

1433), Infante Henrique of Portugal (1394-1460), nicknamed Prince Henry the Navigator, financed a number of missions to explore African shores. Acting as a sponsor, he wanted to reach the gold-bearing regions of the Gulf of Guinea. However, the ships he financed did not go further than Cape Verde, which was reached in 1445. After his death 15 years later, there was a decline in the number of expeditions for several years, and the Equator was only reached in 1475. It was not until King John II (1455-1495) was crowned in 1481 that explorations resumed, now becoming a high priority for the Crown. It was under his reign that the mouth of the Congo River and the coasts of Namibia were explored between 1483 and 1486 and, three years later, that Bartolomeu Dias (1450-1500) rounded the Cape of Storms, which would subsequently be renamed the Cape of Good Hope.

However, these discoveries would not have been possible without the many advances in navigation that had been made in recent years. Innovations such as the sternpost rudder, the compass, the lateen and the astrolabe led to major changes in navigation and influenced Portuguese navigators. In this way, they developed the caravel between 1420 and 1440. This small ship with a triangular sail and sternpost rudder could carry up to 150 barrels. Its high degree of manoeuvrability and its ability to sail in all winds made it the ship of choice for sailing around Africa and reaching India.

IN SEARCH OF INDIA

In the late 15th century, most knowledge of Asia in Europe came from the writings of Marco Polo (1254-1324), the famous Venetian merchant who had followed the silk route to China. Thanks to his account, Europeans became aware of the mysterious Cathay (the name given to northern China) and Cipangu (Japan), which aroused their curiosity. India, on the other hand, had been known to the Europeans since Antiquity thanks to the conquests of Alexander the Great (356-323 BC). However, they were completely unaware of the exact location of these territories.

When da Gama sailed into the Indian Ocean, he was entering a part of the world that was unknown to the Europeans, and where they thought that they would find many Christians. However, once there the reality facing them was completely different, as there were many more Muslims than they had expected. All their hopes then centred around the mythical kingdom of Prester John, which many people thought was in Ethiopia. By forming an alliance with this kingdom, the Christians hoped to attack the Muslim world from an unexpected angle.

THE EXPEDITIONS

THE FIRST VOYAGE (1497-1499)

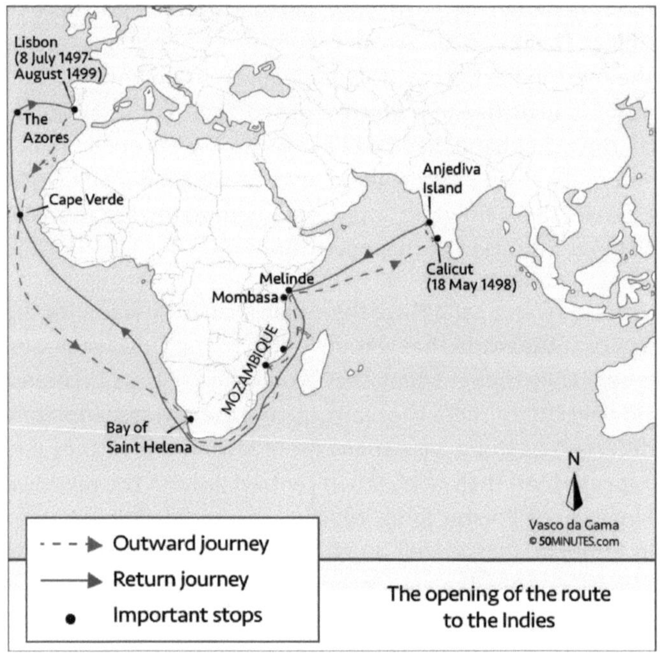

In 1497, the king of Portugal, Manuel I, chose da Gama to lead an expedition with the aim of establishing a maritime route between Portugal and India. While the expedition's aims were of crucial importance, nobody knows why the mission was entrusted to a navigator who was little known up to that point.

Vasco da Gama tasked by Manuel I with discovering India,
engraving by Mauricio José do Carmo Sendim, c. 1839.

On 8 July 1497, da Gama set sail from the estuary of the
Tagus River at the head of four ships. The expedition, which
was financed by the Crown, comprised three caravels and a
supply ship:

- the *São Gabriel*, commanded by da Gama
- the *São Rafael*, commanded by Vasco's brother Paulo da
  Gama (died in 1499)
- the *Berrio*, commanded by Nicolau Coelho (died in 1504).

When the four ships weighed anchor, there were around
160 men on board, as well as some pieces of artillery and
samples of spices, gold and pearls, which were needed so
that the indigenous inhabitants that they would encounter
could tell them where to get more.

The journey to India lasted 11 months, but the crossing was interspersed with various stops in order to repair the ships and pick up water and other supplies. On 27 July, the expedition reached Cape Verde, where the crew were able to rest. Eight days later, the four ships set sail for the south-west and the high seas. The wind pushed the Portuguese ships within a few hundred miles of the Brazilian coasts, until da Gama decided to set a new course towards the south-east. In this way, he strayed from the itinerary followed a few years earlier by Bartolomeu Dias, who had sailed down the African coast in order to reach the Cape of Good Hope. Da Gama's route instead relied on the trade winds that were present in the Atlantic Ocean.

THE IMPORTANCE OF TRADE WINDS

Trade winds are winds which are present in the northern and southern parts of the Atlantic. Without understanding why they were there, the Portuguese followed their movement. When da Gama realised that the trade winds blew from the south-east to the north-west in the southern hemisphere, he decided to avoid adverse winds by moving away from the African coast and sailing to the west.

After sailing on the high seas for three months with no coastline in sight, on 8 November the ships drew alongside the bay of Saint Helena, to the north of the Cape of Good Hope. On 22 November, the ships rounded the cape. Shortly afterwards, the supply ship was burnt off the coast of South

Africa and the remaining provisions were divided among the remaining ships, which could now begin sailing up towards India. On their way, the crew stopped twice in Mozambique, where they met the local inhabitants, the Bantus, for the first time. These stopovers were also an opportunity to fill the holds of the ships with fresh water and fruit in order to combat scurvy, which was affecting many of the sailors. In the remaining three months of the crossing, da Gama reached Mombasa (a port in Kenya) in April, where the crew received a hostile reception, and then Melinde (now known as Malindi, a town in Kenya), where they were given a friendlier welcome. The captain welcomed a Gujarati pilot on board. Thanks to his valuable knowledge, the three ships could sail through the islands and reefs until they reached the Malabar Coasts. On 18 May 1498, the expedition finally arrived in Calicut.

For three months, the Portuguese caravels remained off the coast of Calicut, a Hindu city which attracted many Muslim merchants. However, da Gama was very wary due to the sometimes frosty welcome he had received from the local population. The situation did not improve when the Muslim merchants, who looked unfavourably on the arrival of the Portuguese in their place of business, described them as uncivilised privateers to the Zamorin. The crew therefore needed to wait for tensions to subside before they could set foot on land. They nonetheless still managed to fill the holds of their ships with exotic goods and pearls. The situation worsened further when da Gama told the Zamorin that he wanted to leave several men in Calicut. However, this was nothing compared to the tension that arose when each camp took hostages in order to put pressure on its adversaries. The caravels finally fled on 29 August.

Vasco da Gama received by the Zamorin Samutiri Manavikraman, engraving by Mauricio José do Carmo Sendim, c. 1839.

Three weeks later, the expedition reached Anjediva Island in the Arabian Sea, where the crew stopped before embarking on the return leg of their journey towards Europe. However, this did not bring a return to calm: the descent towards the Cape of Good Hope was one of the most difficult parts of the expedition, and the crew, which had been decimated by scurvy, was forced to abandon the *São Rafael* due to a shortage of men. They rounded the cape on 20 March 1499, and on 10 July Nicolau Coelho was the first to arrive in Portugal. Da Gama was forced to stop in the Azores in order to care for his sick brother, but his efforts were in vain. He only returned at the end of August.

THE SECOND VOYAGE (1502-1503)

In 1502, Manuel I once again chose da Gama to undertake a new expedition to the Indian Ocean and India. This time, he had a completely different aim: to subdue, by will or by force, the African kings and the Zamorin of Calicut.

On 10 February 1502, 20 ships set sail in the direction of Africa. Once there, da Gama had to use force to subdue the King of Kilwa (an island that is part of modern-day Tanzania), who became the first to pay tribute to the Spanish Crown, while the King of Melinde accepted the Portuguese sailors' proposition more willingly.

The situation in India was completely different. The expedition led by Cabral from 1500 to 1501 had had to deal with numerous attacks from Calicut, including the seizure of its trading post by Muslim merchants. As such, the expedition to India was more of a punitive mission against Calicut and the Muslim merchants. Before the Malabar Coast had been reached, the tone for the expedition had already been set: the Portuguese needed to be merciless. In September, when they intercepted a Muslim ship returning from Mecca and carrying pilgrims, they showed their cruelty for the first time. Da Gama refused the tributes offered by the captives in exchange for their lives and gave the order to sink the ship with its passengers on board. The atrocities did not stop there. In October 1502, the Portuguese arrived in India and unleashed their wrath on Calicut in reprisal for the destruction of the trading post set up by Cabral in 1500 and the killing of its 50 members. As the Zamorin refused to pay compensation, around 50 Indian fishermen were captured, tortured and then hanged in front of the city. After this, the Portuguese artillery fired on Calicut and da Gama's men hanged a number of Brahmans (Hindu religious figures belonging to the highest caste).

The crew then went to the outskirts of Cochin and Kannur (to the south and north of Calicut respectively), where the end of their voyage proved more peaceful. Indeed, these two cities wanted to escape from the Zamorin's authority and had made valuable connections with Cabral during his first voyage. Da Gama decided to make the most of these favourable relations and set up a second trading post or *feitoria*, which he established in Cochin. The city then became the hub of the Portuguese expeditions until the trading post in Goa was founded. In spite of a triumphant return to Portugal within 1600 tons of spices, da Gama was removed from the colonial enterprise because of his cruelty during the expedition.

THE *FEITORIAS*

The commercial organisation of the Portuguese Empire was based on *feitorias*. These were trading posts managed by a royal officer, with the aim of buying goods from indigenous inhabitants and then transporting them to Lisbon, where they would be received by the *Casa da Índia*.

THE LAST VOYAGE (1524)

Around 20 years after da Gama's second voyage, the Portuguese Empire in the Indian Ocean had developed considerably: a number of *feitorias* had been built and Portugal now controlled the most important maritime routes for the spice trade, with the exception of the Red Sea.

PORTUGUESE INDIA

Portuguese India (*Estado da Índia*), which refers to the Portuguese Empire in Asia, comprised Portuguese establishments from the Cape of Good Hope to Timor (an island in the Indonesian archipelago). These establishments were administered by a viceroy or governor belonging to the Portuguese upper classes (*fidalgos*). They were tasked with representing royal authority in these regions and administering them, and they also took on the role of military leader if needed.

In 1523, da Gama was recalled to the Court by Manuel I's successor, King John III (1502-1557), while other countries were beginning to jeopardise Portuguese interests in this part of the world. The first circumnavigation of the globe by the Spanish marked their arrival in the Moluccas, a group of islands which were rich in cloves and nutmeg and where the Portuguese had been present since 1510. There was also the incompetence of the Portuguese governor, Duarte de Menezes (c. 1488-c. 1539), in the management of the *Estado da Índia*. Furthermore, at this time, corruption was omnipresent in the empire. All these elements led John III to appoint da Gama viceroy and send him back to Asia.

Da Gama weighed anchor in April 1524 at the head of a fleet of 14 ships and arrived in Goa, which had become the capital of the empire in the East, in September. Once there, he appointed new officials, including his sons, to key posts in the administration. However, three months after his arrival, he died of malaria on Christmas Eve, before he had been able to reform the administration.

IMPACT

A NEW ORGANISATION OF TRADE

After the Portuguese arrived in Asia, the organisation of their trade was gradually implemented. This was based on three elements:

- The *feitorias* were the trading posts set up along the edge of the Indian Ocean, from Mozambique to the Moluccas. They served as purchasing centres for exotic goods. Consequently, Portuguese ships went there to pick up supplies before returning to Lisbon.
- The *Casa da Índia* was the centre for receiving products sent from Asia. It role was to control all trade, meaning imports and exports, as well as the checking and distribution of goods.
- The *Feitoria de Flandres* in Antwerp was the last level of the organisation of trade. This city was one of the main financial centres of the time and many goods were taken there in order to find buyers. In exchange for these exotic goods, the ships brought back products that were needed in their society, such as grains, textiles, metals and currency.

NEW POWER RELATIONSHIPS IN THE MEDITERRANEAN

The incidents which occurred during the first Portuguese expeditions in Asia had a direct impact in the Muslim world. In the Eastern Mediterranean, hostilities between the

Christian nations and the Ottoman Empire were rekindled, and the Sultan of the Mamluks in Egypt threatened Portugal with reprisals if hostilities continued on the Malabar Coast. Faced with these mounting tensions, Manuel I decided to increase his presence in the Indian Ocean by sending a viceroy or a governor there, and to build fortresses in key locations in order to guarantee trade and remove competition from the Muslims. This defensive policy resulted in the Portuguese expansion in Asia, the establishment of a series of trading posts and the domination over the main spice routes. Da Gama was therefore at the root of the process of colonisation in Asia, which only came to an end in the 20th century.

The ousting of a significant proportion of the Muslim merchants in the Indian Ocean by the Portuguese had indirect consequences for the commercial health of Venice, whose trade was primarily based on spices transported from the East by Muslim merchants. Pushed out of this lucrative trade, apart from some incoming goods from the Red Sea, which remained outside Portuguese control, the maritime city saw a decline in its revenues from trade. It only regained access to the spice trade at the end of the century.

THE CHRISTIANISATION OF INDIA

Shortly after the establishment of the first trading posts, mendicant orders of the Catholic Church landed in India. Franciscans, Dominicans, Augustinians and Jesuits had the mission of evangelising the local populations, a duty that the Portuguese Crown should have carried out alongside the

Church but which was delegated to its religious orders. The most active of these was the Society of Jesus, represented in particular by Saint Francis Xavier (1506-1552). Known as the "Apostle of the Indies", Francis was considered to be the leading Jesuit missionary in Asia, and until his death constantly preached the Gospel in various regions, including Japan, China and India.

Starting in the second half of the century, Goa became the hub of Catholicism, with religious buildings for the four orders. Described as the "Rome of the East", it became home to the first archdiocese in Asia.

A NEW KNOWLEDGE OF THE WORLD

Soon after establishing the maritime route leading to the Indian Ocean, the Portuguese discovered Brazil (1500) and began exploring Japan in the 16th century. In order to pursue their exploration of this part of the world, the Portuguese felt the need to obtain new tools to make their expedition easier. From then on, cartographers decided to put new Portuguese discoveries on their maps. The best example of this is the Cantino planisphere (1502), which brought together the knowledge acquired during the first voyages towards the East: it therefore featured Brazil, the entire African continent, India and Insulindia (Maritime Southeast Asia). This map, which was displayed in the *Casa da Mina da Índia* in Lisbon and was of inestimable value for the time, was copied by an Italian spy and then taken to Italy, where it provided valuable knowledge on the state of the world.

SUMMARY

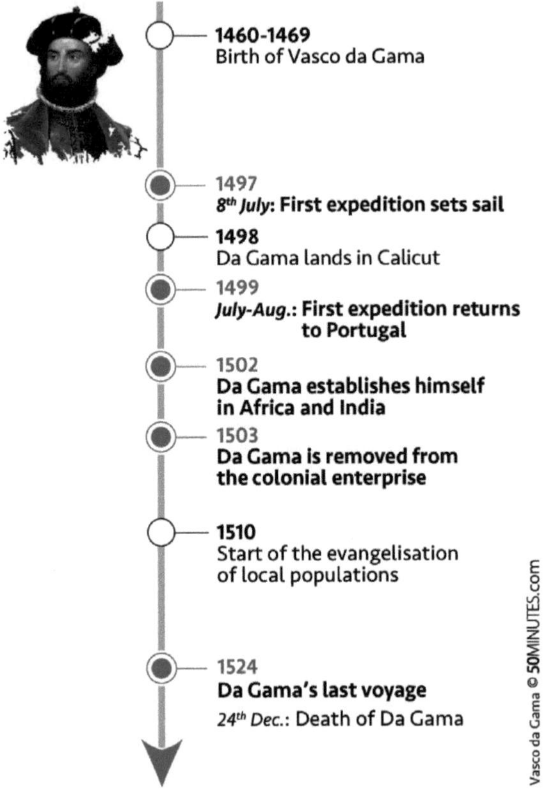

- Vasco da Gama was born in either 1460 or 1469 in Sines, Portugal.
- In 1497, the Portuguese Crown chose him to lead an expedition with the aim of discovering a maritime route

leading to the Indies.

- On 8 July, he set sail from the estuary of the Tagus River with four ships. He sailed around Africa, reached the Cape of Good Hope and then sailed back up the Western coast of Africa. The expedition reached various city-states which were sometimes hostile to the travellers. The crew finally arrived in Calicut in May 1498. Although relations with the local leader were tense, they obtained the coveted spices, but did not encounter the Christians they had been hoping to find.

- As his voyage had been a great success, he was once again chosen by the king to lead a new expedition, this time with the aim of extending Portuguese domination to Calicut.

- He left on 10 February 1502 and managed to establish himself in East Africa and India, and to eliminate some of the competition from Muslim merchants. As he had had no qualms about using force to achieve this, da Gama fell into disgrace and only returned to the Court in the late 1510s.

- His third voyage to India had the aim of defending the interests of the Crown. He was appointed viceroy and given the mission of putting an end to corruption and protecting the trading posts. The reforms that had been implemented had led to dissatisfaction among the colonists, which needed to be quelled.

- Three months after his arrival, da Gama died of malaria in Cochin.

- Based on the principles of thalassocracy (the government of a nation which controls large expanses of the seas), the *Estado da Índia* was built along the edges of the Indian

Ocean with trading posts and forts. The Muslims could not compete with the spread of the Portuguese, and were gradually pushed out of the spice trade.

- The arrival of the Portuguese in Asia resulted in major political upheaval in that part of the world. Some African and Asian countries and city-states saw an alliance with the Portuguese as an opportunity to gain the upper hand in their local claims or, conversely, to harm Portuguese interests.
- This maritime route also paved the way for the evangelising missions undertaken by the various religious orders of the Church. Starting in 1510, missionaries arrived in Asia in order to evangelise local populations. In the early 16th century, Goa became an archdiocese where the four religious orders gathered.

We want to hear from you!
Leave a comment on your online library
and share your favourite books on social media!

FIND OUT MORE

BIBLIOGRAPHY

- Astier, A. (2010) *Histoire de l'Inde*. Paris: Eyrolles.
- Didier, H. (2005) *Découvertes de l'Inde : de Vasco de Gama à Lord Mountbatten*. Paris: Kailash Éditions.
- Disney, A.R. (2009) *A History of Portugal and the Portuguese Empire: From Beginnings to 1807*. Cambridge: Cambridge University Press.
- Elbi, M. and Elbi, I. (2007) Vasco Da Gama. *World Exploration*, volume 1. Oxford: Oxford University Press. pp. 341-342.
- Fritze, R.H. (2005) Gama, Vasco Da. *Renaissance & Early Modern Era (1454-1600)*. Ipswich, Massachusetts: Salem Press. pp. 365-368.
- Grimbli, S. (2001) *Atlas of Exploration*. London: Fitzroy Dearborn Publishers.
- Labourdette, J.-F. (2000) *Histoire du Portugal*. Paris: Fayard.
- Virmani, A. (2012) *Atlas historique de l'Inde*. Paris: Autrement.

ADDITIONAL SOURCES

- Cliff, N. (2013) *The Last Crusade: The Epic Voyages of Vasco da Gama*. New York: Harper Perennial.
- Crowley, R. (2016) *Conquerors: How Portugal Forged the First Global Empire*. London: Faber & Faber.

ICONOGRAPHIC SOURCES

- Portrait of Vasco da Gama by Antoine Maurin, c. 1835. Royalty-free reproduction picture.
- *Vasco da Gama tasked by Manuel I with discovering India*, engraving by Mauricio José do Carmo Sendim, c. 1839. © National Library of Portugal.
- *Vasco da Gama received by the Zamorin Samutiri Manavikraman*, engraving by Mauricio José do Carmo Sendim, c. 1839. © National Library of Portugal.

LITERATURE

- De Camões, L. (2008) *The Lusíads*. Oxford: Oxford University Press.